Be Real About Guidance

Understanding the will of God in your life

Don Double

with Tim Jones

New Wine Press

New Wine Press
PO Box 17
Chichester PO20 6YB
England

Other books by Don Double

Life in a new dimension
Live like a king
The five facts of life
It's the greatest day you ever lived
The positive power of the fear of God
What to do in a storm
Victory over depression
Healing the Jesus Way

Also

It's a wonderful new life
Don Double's biography by Eileen Thompson

All scripture quotations, unless otherwise indicated, are from the New King James Version.
Copyright © 1982 Thomas Nelson, Inc.

Scripture quotations marked NIV are from the Holy Bible, New International Version.
Copyright © 1973, 1978, International Bible Society.
Published by Hodder & Stoughton.

ISBN 1 874367 01 9

Typeset by CRB Typesetting Services, Ely, Cambs.
Printed by Richard Clay Ltd, Bungay Suffolk.

Contents

Everyday Guidance

Chapter 1

Let's Go For a Walk

Guidance is a very simple thing. If you've been seeking God and have not been able to get clear guidance, you might disagree with me. I hope to show you in this book, just how easy it is to know the will of God for your life. I believe that one of the reasons people have problems with guidance is that they try to make it too complex. If knowing God's will for your day is complicated then there is something very definitely wrong, because it should be simple. It is all to do with walking with God.

People try to tell me guidance is not simple and I don't understand or appreciate their difficulties. They say 'if you had a husband/wife like mine, (or parents, or children, or circumstances) you wouldn't say that.' But look at Enoch; he walked with God for three hundred years (Genesis 5:21–24). He certainly had a wife and many children (Genesis 5:22) and yet he was still able to walk with God. It doesn't matter what our circumstances are, it is possible for everyone to walk with God.

Further on in Genesis we read of Noah, another man who walked with God. Noah made some mistakes but he still maintained his walk with God. People who make mistakes are not disqualified from walking with God. You too may make mistakes, but it is still possible to go on with God, so don't stop.

I have met people who have been most sincere and diligent in seeking to walk with God and to obey His leading and guidance. Sadly something has gone wrong in their lives, usually to do with a guidance issue, and their relationship with God has grown cold and distant. Sadder still has been the way in which that wound has affected everything they do, often making them indecisive people.

I knew a young lady, in her late twenties, who began to feel a bit 'on the shelf'. She began to pray, asking God for a husband. As she did, she felt the Lord say that a man would come to her house who would ask for a cup of water; he would be the man who was going to be her husband! Some time later a man turned up at the house and he asked for a cup of water and of course she got very excited. They became friends but they certainly didn't fall in love. Eventually she could not wait any longer, and she told him, 'The Lord has told me that you've got to marry me!' The man replied, 'But the Lord hasn't told me I've got to marry you.' Their relationship didn't last long after that. The result was that the girl was badly wounded by the experience but she couldn't lay down what she thought God had said to her.

It's important to be real. I hope you can realise and learn quickly that guidance is not infallible and the reason for that is because we're involved in it. We're human beings and we can make mistakes, and so whenever you get direction hold it lightly.

Throughout the Old Testament, if the children of Israel walked with God, everything went right. If they did wrong in the sight of God things went wrong. Now that is very quickly summing up the whole of Old Testament history but it is the truth. If the Israelites walked with God everything went according to plan, they won every battle they went into, they were invincible. However, they couldn't win a battle, however hard they tried, if they didn't walk with God. It is a principle that every Christian needs in their lives. If you walk with God, things go right. If you don't walk with God things go wrong.

In the New Testament walking with God is called 'walking in the Spirit'. When something seems to go right have you heard someone say, 'I must have been in the Spirit!' It implies that the rest of their life is out of the Spirit. Some people get the idea that being 'led by the Spirit' is something weird or wonderful; they seem to think that it is something they will achieve occasionally, perhaps once a year, if they try really hard. I don't believe that's right, that is a negative attitude; we should live and walk in the Spirit every moment of every day.

Even worse than just making it occasionally are the people who use 'led by the Spirit' as a cover for their own selfishness. 'The Spirit hasn't told me to ...' or 'I don't feel led' can be abusing the Holy Spirit and is not a holy attitude.

> *'For as many as are led by the Spirit of God, these are sons of God.'*
>
> (Romans 8:14).

People who are living under God's direction and guidance are manifesting their sonship. Those who do their own thing and go their own way, although they are sons of God, are not living like sons of God at all. Our great example of this godly principle is the Lord Jesus Christ, The Son of God. The way He walked is the way we should walk (1 John 2:6). That is what the issue of guidance is all about, just walking as He walked.

Jesus said (read this very carefully),

> *'I am able to do nothing from Myself – independently, of My own accord – but as I am taught by God and as I get His orders. [I decide as I am bidden to decide. As the voice comes to Me, so I give a decision.] Even as I hear, I judge and My judgement is right (just, righteous), because I do not seek* or *consult My own will – I have no desire to do what is pleasing to Myself, My own aim, My own purpose – but only the will* and *pleasure of the Father Who sent Me.'*
>
> (John 5:30 Amplified Bible)

I can't think of anything simpler than going for a walk with someone. Just imagine this situation: I have invited George for a walk and as we are getting ready to go out, George says, 'Where shall we go Don?' 'I don't know, where do you suggest?' George suggests a walk into the hills and as I do not know the way I follow him. I have no clues where we are going, so I have to trust George. He's familiar with the area so he leads the way. As long as I let George lead there is no problem at all. It's easy for me, all I've got to do is follow where he goes. But if, half way, I said to George, 'Let's go this way,' problems will begin. As I argue about the direction to go, George may allow me to go my own way, knowing that very soon I will be lost.

The only reason I'm lost is because I wanted my own way; that's the first sin that any person ever commits. The Bible says, *'All we like sheep have gone astray; we have turned, every one, to his own way; and the LORD has laid on Him the iniquity of us all.'* (Isaiah 53:6)

If you want your own way, you cannot be guided. The two don't go together. If you want to walk with God you must be willing to walk God's way. Get that principle working in your life, make it part of your lifestyle and you will have no problem with getting guidance.

If you want to walk with God you must be willing to walk God's way.

'Can two walk together, unless they are agreed?' (Amos 3:3). You can't walk together unless you are

11

in agreement. If you ask God to show you the way, you've got to walk God's way. *'He has shown you, O man, what is good. And what does the Lord require of you but to do justly to love mercy, and to walk humbly with your God.'* (Micah 6:8). To receive guidance you must be humble, you've got to lay down your own will, your own desires, your own way and be humble, wanting to walk God's way. Guidance is a relationship with the Lord.

Often when you agree to walk with God, He will take you along surprising paths. It does take faith to walk with Him, but that is exciting because it is then that you see miracles take place before your eyes. An example of this happened to me on one occasion when I was conducting a crusade in Zimbabwe.

The team and I were in the north of the country, in the town of Victoria Falls, which is near the famous waterfalls. The accommodation that had been arranged for us fell through before we arrived, and the only alternative we could find was a log cabin in a safari park, some way out of town. When we got to Victoria Falls we drove past a hotel, and as we did, I felt a very strong impression that this was where we were to stay. Then I saw a large sign on the building, 'CASINO.' This caused me a problem – was it right for us as the team conducting this major Christian outreach, to stay in a casino? Would the safari lodge be 'safer'?

We decided to find somewhere else for lunch and then went to see the famous waterfalls, but all the time I felt God was saying 'stay in that hotel, stay in that hotel.' So, while the rest of the team stayed to see more of the Falls, the local crusade coordinator and I went back to the hotel to see what was there. We found that the casino was quite separate from the hotel and that there were rooms available; we agreed that this was what God had provided for us and booked in.

Later, whilst the team were getting settled in, my colleague Peter Gammons went to investigate the facilities. After several minutes he came back very excited; one of the largest outreach teams in Africa were holding a secret conference for their executive committee in the hotel. Amongst the people gathered for this meeting was a Ugandan church leader who I had been trying to contact for some time, concerning a crusade we were planning in his country. When Peter said that, I knew then that God had supernaturally led us to the hotel. He knew exactly where this man was and He arranged for us to met in a most unusual setting. When you allow God to lead you can relax, God has prepared the way ahead and knows what He is doing; all we have to do is follow Him.

There are many people who know about God, but don't really know Him. Perhaps you are like that; you do not have an intimate relationship with Him. As you have read about walking with God as a relationship, you have realised that this is something foreign to you. If that describes you then it is time to do something about it. Don't delay any longer because it is God's will that everyone knows Him intimately and begins to walk with Him. Just knowing about God and learning the facts about him is not enough, you've got to know Him personally.

If you don't know God, it is time to act. What follows is a prayer that is the beginning of that relationship. If you know that what I have written describes you, pray the prayer. Then, tell someone what you have done who can encourage you further and help you to develop your relationship with God. If you don't know anyone that can do that, please write to me and I and my team will help you.

'Lord God, thank you for being interested in me. I want a friendship with you. I realise that you have made that possible through the death and resurrection of your Son, Jesus Christ.

I confess that I have sinned, and accept that through the blood that Jesus shed on the Cross, I can be forgiven. I repent and turn from my sin. I open my life to you and ask you to come, take control of it and be my Lord. I recognise you to be the authority in my life.

Thank you, Father God, for hearing my prayer.

Amen.'

Chapter 2

Relax, God Loves You

Now that we have established that God does want to guide us, there is an important principle we need to get into our lives. The best way I can communicate it, is to ask you to think about a car. The principle is very simple, but many people miss it completely: a moving car is a lot easier to direct than one that is stationary!

I meet many people who have the idea that they are not going to do anything until God directs them. Sadly, those people become frustrated because they are not achieving anything. We need to be on the move, we need to be active and the result will see God's plan for us unfold as we step out in faith. If you begin to do what the Bible says, you'll learn to hear God's voice and to recognise Him when He speaks.

'Today, if you will hear His voice, Do not harden

your hearts as in the rebellion.' (Hebrews 3:15). One of the reasons people struggle with knowing God's will is that at some point they heard God speak, but they hardened their hearts, they rebelled against the voice of God; now they can't hear God's voice. Do you know why? Because God has nothing else to say until they have obeyed what He's said before. Ignoring God is one of the biggest hindrances to guidance. If you are wondering why you can't hear God's voice go back and make sure that you've done the last thing He told you to do. Then you'll begin to hear His voice clearly again.

God can only speak to faith. Read through Hebrews chapters 3 and 4 and you will discover that the children of Israel did not believe God, which caused them serious problems. Like the Israelites, if you're not in faith you'll never hear the voice of God. Doubt or unbelief will produce the following: 'Is it me or is it the Lord? Is it the devil or is it me? Is it the Lord, or is it me?' Have you ever had that conversation with yourself? Doubt always confuses your ability to hear God. Faith hears God's voice and does not doubt it; you have to trust the Lord.

> *'Trust in the LORD with all your heart, and lean not on your own understanding; in all your ways acknowledge Him, and He shall direct your paths.'*
>
> (Proverbs 3:5–6)

I think that verse is tremendous but such a challenge. If we are trusting Him with all our heart, we deliberately do not lean on our own understanding and we acknowledge Him in everything we do. Every tick of the clock I want Jesus to be Lord of my life; with every breath I breathe I want to do His will. I want to acknowledge Him in all that I do. If I do, He has made a promise, He'll direct my paths and make them straight.

Guidance comes from our relationship with the Lord, not from our common sense. Put another way, guidance should not come from the fruit of tree of the knowledge of good and evil. You see, it was never God's intention for us to know good and evil (Genesis 2:17). While most people understand that it wasn't God's will for us to know evil, they forget that it was not God's will for us to know good either. He wanted us to know Himself. The Bible says God wanted us to eat from the tree of life (Genesis 2:9). Adam and Eve were free to eat from that tree but not from the tree of the knowledge of good and evil. I believe the tree of life represented the person of the Lord Jesus and it is partaking of Him and of His life that is the source of our guidance.

When God speaks there is nothing else to say. All we should do is to just get on and do what He has said, and the quicker we do it, the better. Too much tension and confusion is caused in Christians' lives by worrying about what God has said; they get into an unnecessary state of anxiety. Philippians 4:6–7 says, *'Be anxious for nothing, but in everything by prayer and supplication, with thanksgiving, let your requests be made known to God; and the peace of God, which surpasses all understanding, will guard your hearts and minds through Christ Jesus.'* Worry is sin, and can have serious consequences; a lot of people have become physically unwell directly through worrying. Others have become terribly depressed and fearful, as they began to worry about guidance. Sadly, it becomes a vicious circle as no one can be guided once they get into that state. They go round and round, getting more worried and more upset at their lack of guidance. How do you break the circle? By coming to faith and knowing that God loves you, not because somebody else tells you so, but by really knowing deep down God's love for you.

I remember driving down the M1 several years ago, when God spoke to me and said 'Don, why won't you let me love you the way I want to?' 'Lord I thought I was doing pretty well. I thought that I was revelling in your love.' But the Lord showed me that He wanted to love me even more and it was up to me to let Him love me. God loves me and knowing that makes it easy to be daily in God's will. That is because I know that God wants me to be in His will even more than I do. God does not tease us nor does He tempt us; the Bible says He loves us. This is a place of security, knowing that God wants me in His will more than I do.

However, that does produce a question. Do you want to be in His will? I can't answer for you, but the fact that you are reading this book indicates you are open to hear. For myself, I want to be in God's will more than anything else in the entire world. I can think of nowhere else I want to be, other than in the centre of God's will. If God wants me to be in His will, and I want to be in His will, what is stopping me? Nothing at all. Simple isn't it? I believe I am always in His will until He shows me I'm out of it. So the responsibility is on Him to lead me, not on me to work out if I'm in or out of His will. I have settled it, and constantly pray, 'If I go to take one step outside of your will, please stop me Lord.' That means I no longer have to worry about the will of God, because of my commitment to Him. My prayer of commitment has put the responsibility on Him to lead and guide me. Often we put too much responsibility onto man and send people away struggling, sweating and toiling. People need to relax and just spend time walking with the Lord, and then let direction for their lives come out of that place of rest.

Keeping the Peace

'Let the peace of God rule in your hearts, since as members of one body you are called to peace.' (Colossians 3:15 NIV) This is a very popular 'guidance' scripture, which is often misunderstood. The Amplified Bible, uses the word umpire, instead of rule: *'Let the peace of God be the umpire.'* If your peace goes, stop straight away. Don't go on, stop and find out what's gone wrong and get back into God's will. I trust God that He will not wait until I've taken ten steps before disturbing my peace. Rather as I lift my foot to go in the wrong direction He will stop me

before I put it down. That's the kind of God we serve, if we can believe it.

In cricket the umpire plays an important role. The fielding team appeal to the umpire, 'Howzat?!' Is the batsman in or out? The umpire doesn't say a word, all he does is he raises a finger and that person is out. It's no good arguing, the batsman has got to turn round and walk back to the pavilion. That's the end of the matter, the umpire's decision is final. This is what the peace of God should do in our hearts. If our 'peace' is disturbed then it means the umpire has put his finger up and you're out of God's will. You can argue, you can reason, but it won't alter your peace if you have stepped out of His will. Even if you find someone who will sympathise with you, when you go back into God's presence the umpire's finger is still up. The only thing to do is to turn to God and ask how you have got out, and then do something about it.

It says in Romans 8:31 (NIV), *'What, then, shall we say in response to this? If God is for us, who can be against us?'* **God is for you, Hallelujah!** The devil can try to oppose us but he is not going to win; he'll lose every time and one day everyone will know that he's lost. Can people be against us? If God is for you, there is no one that can stand against you. That even includes the times when you make mistakes. God is still for you. He doesn't withdraw because you make a mistake; He still loves you and cares for you. He'll do everything He can to show you your mistake and bring you back into His love. God cares for you and loves you.

An old song we used to sing says:

'He loves me when I'm right and He loves me when I'm wrong.'

That's a tremendous truth.

> *'If a man has a hundred sheep, and one of them goes astray, does he not leave the ninety-nine and go to the mountains to seek the one that is straying? And if he should find it, assuredly, I say to you, he rejoices more over that sheep than over the ninety-nine that did not go astray. Even so it is not the will of your Father who is in heaven that one of these little ones should perish.'*
>
> (Matthew 18:12–14)

This parable has been the basis of thousands of successful gospel messages, but re-read it in the context of the whole chapter. This parable is to do with staying in God's will. It talks about sheep and one that wanders off from the fold. You could well take it that the one who is lost, has lost his guidance, and has missed the way. It shows you the concern of the shepherd, the great Shepherd of our souls, our Father God. He's concerned about that one sheep and wants to find it and bring it back into His fold. This is a wonderful security for me, if I wander off I believe God is so concerned, that He's going to do everything He can to bring me back to His way. When our faith knows God loves us like this, we then have a concept of God, not with a big stick trying to catch us out, but of the loving Father. You can relax and let the Lord lead you. Isn't that great?

Don't get all tensed up, expect God to lead you. When I got up this morning I didn't say, 'Now, Lord I want you to lead me through this day; I want you to be very careful Lord, that I don't make any mistakes. You know how weak and hopeless I am!' No, I woke up and said 'Hallelujah, Lord' and worshipped Him a little and shared in fellowship with Him, and then got out of bed expecting Him to lead me and as a result, today, as everyday, can be THE GREATEST DAY I'VE EVER LIVED!

Chapter 3

Are Your Ears Blocked?

When considering the issue of being led by God it is important to realize that our attitudes must be right. If we have wrong ideas and expectations we won't hear what God says, or even worse we'll mishear His guidance. In the following chapter I want us to examine our hearts and see what attitudes we hold that could stop us from hearing God.

Trustworthy Words

God is never 'unscriptural' in the guidance He gives. You'll never get any guidance that is contrary to the Word of God. He will never ask you to do things that contradict or deny what He has said in His Word.

When thinking about guidance many people make a distinction between the two major Greek words for 'word', *logos* and *rhema*. They regard *rhema* as a 'now' word, something that can be specifically applied in their current situation; *logos* describes, for them, the whole general counsel of God, particularly what is recorded in the Bible. We're living in days when people are very keen to get *rhema* words. I'm not against people being directed by prophetic 'words,' but there is one very important condition. The true *rhema* word never has more authority than the written word, and will always be scriptural. Let the Bible be your guiding principle in any direction that you receive.

In Colossians 3:16 it says *'Let the word of Christ dwell in you richly ... '* If you let God's Word dwell in you richly you'll have a better chance of making wise decisions, than if you just take little snippets every so often. Let the Word of God dwell in you, and become your lifestyle.

How to be Deceived

It is important to know that if you seek guidance on a matter that the Word of God has already spoken clearly about, you open yourself to deception. I've met many people who tried to get guidance about 'the will of God' when the Word of God has made it very plain what God thinks about the issue. When they tried to act on 'guidance' they preferred, the result has always been disastrous. Let me give you a real-life example:

I counselled a couple who asked me for help; they weren't husband and wife but were both married and living with their partners, who were also Christians. This couple were absolutely convinced that God had told them that they were meant for each other and that they were going to be married one day. They believed that in some mysterious way God was going to sort it all out and make it possible, both scripturally and legally. The man told me that he used to take this woman to church, leaving his wife to get to the same church by some other way! I could not convince them that anything they were doing was wrong. It was clear that they had allowed themselves to be deceived and now were controlled by a spirit of deception.

How did this situation happen? They ignored God's written word, in preference for a so called 'rhema' word. As a result they were bound so that they couldn't hear the truth anymore. God's Word had already spoken, *'What God has joined together, let not man separate.'* (Matthew 19:6). They had both made vows before Almighty God that they were going to love their partners 'til death do us part.' To seek God for guidance whether they should have another partner, was in truth saying to the devil, 'Please deceive us.'

If you ask God to guide you on something that His Word is already clear and plain on then you open yourself up to all the powers of darkness and can become controlled by deception. I hope that you really understand that; embed that truth into your life. If God's Word says something, God will never say anything different for your situation.

Are You Unstable?

> *'A double-minded man* [is] *unstable in all his ways.'*

> (James 1:8)

You can easily spot a double-minded man: every time you see him, he has a new idea or project. He is excited about something different from the last time you met him. He never accomplishes what he sets out to do, yet he has always got something new, which 'God, is telling him to do.' In truth the double-minded person is always changing his mind, but would never admit it.

God never changes His mind. Aren't you glad you've got a God like that? He knows what's right, the first time. He never has to have an emergency committee meeting of Father, Son and Holy Spirit to decide the next move, He's already there.

A double-minded person is an unstable person and cannot be led or guided. You can only lead a person who is single-minded. That's why Matthew 6:22 (KJV) is full of such promise: *'The light of the body is the eye: if therefore thine eye be single, thy whole body shall be full of light.'* That means we will be full of God's guidance because Psalm 119:105 describes God's word as a lamp and a light.

Conforming to God's Will

To be able to obey the will of God you must be honest with yourself. Be real about what's going on

26

inside you, in your heart and your mind. You may need to take time to see what's happening inside, so that you get your will in line with God's will, and your way matching God's way.

Jesus faced this battle, He was *'in all points tempted as we are,'* (Hebrews 4:15), but He had to come to the place where He prayed, *'Not my will, but Yours, be done'* (Luke 22:42). Jesus in His humanity had a will that had to come into line with His Father's will in heaven. Like us Jesus lived with two wills, His own and His Father's. He did not consult His own will but did the will of His Father in Heaven (John 5:30). He had to fight the same battle of wills that you and I do. Remember that God never takes our will from us, we always have to choose which way to go. God wants us to be free, moral beings.

It is important that we realise the eternal consequences of this battle. Jesus said,

'Not everyone who says to Me, "Lord, Lord," shall enter the kingdom of heaven, but he who does the will of My Father in heaven.'

(Matthew 7:21)

The choice to do what God is bidding us to do will bring a reward, entrance into the Kingdom of heaven.

If you have a struggle with letting God's will rule, spend some time meditating on Romans 12:2: *'And do not be conformed to this world, but be transformed by the renewing of your mind, that you may prove what is that good and acceptable and perfect will of God.'* How are our minds renewed? Well, one way is to *'Let the word of Christ dwell in you richly in all wisdom'* (Colossians 3:16).

In the Amplified Bible's version of John 5:30, Jesus says, *'I am able to do nothing from myself – independently, of My own accord.'* Independence must go. We British people are taught from the cradle to become independent, but it is a terrible sin. You cannot be guided if you have an independent attitude.

Jesus said 'I don't consult my own will, I don't want to do my own thing' (John 5:30). To be at the place where you don't consult your own will means that you have got to die to your will and ambitions. Some of the modern Bible translations use the word 'ambition' in a negative sense, and it is true that ambition can be an evil thing. An overly ambitious person will often be very independent, not caring who they hurt to achieve their desires. In the kingdom of God selfish ambitions must die and we must commit our whole lives to the Lord and to His will. (I would add that I believe that it is good to have goals; Paul talked about aiming for a goal, Philippians 3:14.)

In each moment of every day we should be moving in the centre of God's will. That is the lifestyle God wants in His kingdom. It simply means that you are living under the rule and reign of the Lord Jesus Christ. You are building your life under His authority. He has the government of your life. Some folk ask me silly questions like, 'Can I go to a disco?' or 'Can I go to the cinema?' 'Can I do this, or can I do that?' My answer is always very simple, 'Is God's kingdom there?' 'Is that part of God's kingdom for you?' If it isn't, then don't go near it, because we are to live constantly in the Kingdom.

If you are struggling to know the will of God reread this chapter and carefully consider each point. Are you asking God to guide you when His word already makes clear what He thinks? Are you 'in two minds,' and doubting what God has said. And what about independence? Do you need to get your will in line with God? As your attitudes change believe that you will hear God speak to you clearly, everyday.

Guidance
for
Big Decisions

Chapter 4

Making Big Decisions

Wherever I go people ask me for guidance. One of the motivations for writing this book was to put into print some of the lessons I have learnt about guidance. Often these people ask for guidance concerning big issues like moving house, changing job, getting married; they want help about the life-changing issues which are important to get right. Usually people want me to tell them what to do, but I always try to help them make the decision themselves. In the next two chapters I want show you the steps I take when I face an important decision.

How Big?

First of all we need to remember that it is only a big decision from our perspective. I have discovered that the more mature you get in the Spirit, the smaller problems become, because as you get to be more like the Lord, you see things as He sees them. Realise that there is nothing bigger than God and that whatever decision you have got to make is well within His capabilities. God always has the answer at His fingertips at the very moment you ask Him for help. As I often tell people: God doesn't have any problems, He only has solutions.

Step 1: *Slow down*

> *'Whoever believes will not act hastily.'*
> (Isaiah 28:16 last part)

This verse is speaking prophetically of our Lord's coming, but there is a principle there for us to learn. If you are faced with a big decision, make sure that you are not in a hurry, because you need to come to a place of faith in God. Unbelief will want you to rush, and it is then that people often make mistakes.

I learnt this lesson when Heather and I were furnishing our home. We were believing God to provide what we needed and on the list was a refrigerator. I began to look around to see what was available. In one shop I was offered 12.5% discount, in another 15%. I researched very thoroughly and 15% off was the best deal I could get. All the time I was looking, the Lord said very clearly, 'No, wait. Don't be in a hurry.' I couldn't understand this but found grace to be obedient. Then we went to Plymouth at sale time and in one of the big stores there was a refrigerator marked down with a 33.3% discount. I promptly walked up to the attendant and said 'We'll have that.' He said 'No you won't. The sale doesn't start until nine o'clock on Friday morning. Get in the queue early and you might be lucky.'

We went home and prayed. I believed that the Lord wanted us to have it, but I knew that we were not going to queue all night, so I asked Him to stop anyone else from buying it before Heather could get there. On Friday morning Heather got to the store about twenty minutes before opening and joined the end of a long queue. At 9 a.m. the doors opened and everybody rushed in, but Heather very calmly walked through to the electrical department. As she walked through the doors the assistant looked at Heather, (I'm sure he didn't know her, but this was just the Lord) and said 'Your fridge, madam!' I could easily have bought a fridge with a good saving but by waiting, God gave us the best.

Step 2: *Prayer*

Throughout the gospels, the Lord Jesus Christ spent time in prayer if a major event was going to happen. He found it necessary to have that intimate communion with the Lord before taking the next step. For instance in Matthew 14:23, we read that Jesus had sent the multitudes away, and the disciples out across the Sea of Galilee, and He was alone, at evening. That is around 6 p.m. By verse 25 it is the fourth watch, between 3 a.m. and 6 a.m., so He had been in prayer for at least nine hours. Then Jesus walked over the lake, in the midst of the storm, and greeted the disciples in the boat. I regard that miracle as a major event, and Jesus preceded it by nine hours of prayer. So, when you have got a big decision to make, spend time with God in prayer. Make sure you wait on Him and don't do all the talking either. When I pray, I'm discovering that I'm doing less talking and more listening, because you can hear His voice a lot clearer when you are quiet.

Sometimes your prayers may need fasting added to them. Be aware that fasting does nothing to God. A lot of people think fasting twists God's arm to answer a prayer. That is nonsense; we fast because it does something for us. It allows us to become sensitive to God, more able to hear what God is saying. The elders at Antioch discovered this, and as a result launched a ministry that planted churches all over the known world:

> '*As they ministered to the Lord and fasted, the Holy Spirit said, "Now separate to Me Barnabas and Saul for the work to which I have called them." Then, having fasted and prayed, and laid hands on them, they sent them away.*'
>
> (Acts 13:2–3)

> '*My soul, wait silently for God alone, For my expectation is from Him.*' (Psalm 62:5)

> '*I waited patiently for the LORD; And He inclined to me, And heard my cry.*' (Psalm 40:1)

Waiting on God suggests that we stop rushing to and fro trying to find answers. Press your *pause* button and wait for God to speak. Expect Him to talk to you. It is wonderful to be expectant that God is going to do something for you. Often you will learn far more about God during that waiting period, than if God immediately answered your prayer.

This is a lesson we have learnt when God sends us somewhere on a mission or a crusade. Every crusade is different so we have wait to see which way He's going to work, to find what the keys are that He's going to give us to unlock that particular mission. It is an exciting experience, wondering what He's going to do this time; I have been in full time ministry for over 30 years and there has never been a dull moment working with Him. If you get bored and dull in the things of God, I suggest that you start waiting on Him and let your expectation only come from Him.

Step 3: *There's safety in numbers*

When you have got your guidance and you have begun to see what God wants you to do, check it out. Take your guidance to your pastor or elders, or to trusted Christian friends and share it with them. Tell them what you feel God has shown you.

> *'Where there is no counsel, the people fall; but in the multitude of counsellors there is safety.'*
> (Proverbs 11:14)

If you want to be safe when you are guided in big decisions then be willing to share it with other people. I have found this to be invaluable and I always endeavour to do that when making a big decision.

In 1974 when Heather and I launched out in faith and bought our present house we had to believe God for £25,000. All we had were the proceeds of the house we were selling which was going to be about £10,000. We asked the Lord what we should do and Heather and I felt God give an answer. We then took it to the team, and asked them to seek the Lord, and every one of them witnessed that we had heard correctly. Then everything appeared to go wrong and situation looked impossible. No one would give us a mortgage because we didn't have a regular income; but we had our guidance, and so we kept on believing and would not be moved waiting for God to provide. Then the miracle came. Someone who didn't know us very well, met us at a conference and gave us an interest free loan, for more than we needed so it covered the house purchase and helped us set up home. To have the whole team seek the Lord and to be in unity that this was the right house for us, was exciting.

Step 4: *Get moving!*

My first step was 'Don't rush,' but I want to balance that by saying, once you know what God's will is, get on and **do it**. Don't dilly-dally! If you know that God has spoken, ignore the circumstances you are in, and get on and do the will of God.

> *'For He says: "In an acceptable time I have heard you, and in the day of salvation I have helped you." Behold, now is the accepted time; behold, now is the day of salvation.'*
>
> (2 Corinthians 6:2)

Don't just quote that verse at friends and relatives who need to accept Jesus as Saviour. It is important for us who are asking for guidance. When God opens the door, don't delay going through it.

Coping With Circumstances

I do believe that God can, and does, use circumstances in guiding us, but they should not be our only guide. If your circumstances are contrary to what you believe to be God's will, then you have got to use your faith, and change the circumstances. Too many people allow the circumstances they are in to guide them; the sad truth is that if you let them rule your decision-making, you will end up like Job, in an ash pit, depressed, dejected and deluded.

It is my experience that people pay too much attention to their circumstances. I believe the sons of God should be changing the circumstances instead of letting the world dictate to them what they should do. Look at the life of Jesus; did He allow circumstances to guide Him? No, He changed them.

'And suddenly a great tempest arose on the sea, so that the boat was covered with the waves. But He was asleep. Then His disciples came to Him and awoke Him, saying, "Lord, save us! We are perishing!" But He said to them, "Why are you fearful, O you of little faith?" Then He arose and rebuked the winds and the sea. And there was a great calm.'

(Matthew 8:24–26)

It would have been very nice to let the boat go down, and for them all to get to heaven quicker! I mean, after all, 'absent from the body, present with the Lord,' is far better isn't it? Whilst I meet many people who have this attitude, it is not the attitude Jesus took. He had a job to do, and He was going to finish it. So, He stood up, He rebuked the storm and changed their circumstances. The will of God in this case was for them to get to the other side of the lake, and that is what Jesus did.

Jesus had said to the disciples *'Let's go over to the other side of the lake.'* (Luke 8:22). Jesus knew where He was going and as Oral Roberts once said, 'They could not go under, for going over, with Jesus in the boat!' When Jesus speaks, believe it and know that whatever appearances say, it can be done if you believe and obey. Don't allow anything to stop you.

Look at Jesus' first miracle, which took place at the wedding in Cana. If the same situation happened today, I'm sure several Christians would say, 'Well, the Lord doesn't want us to have any more to drink!

It must be the will of God that we don't drink any more. We'll just have water out of the tap, that will do us nicely.' When Mary involved Jesus He said '*Fill the water pots with water ... and take it to the master of the feast*' (John 2:7,8). He used the circumstances to manifest His glory by changing them. Circumstances are not guidance for you to stay in a negative position but are usually opportunities to use your faith, to display the glory of God, showing yourself and the world what God can do.

By coming out of our circumstances by the power of God, and using our faith in God to change the circumstances, we will bring glory to God. We need to realise that God wants us to do that more often than staying under them and trying to be a good witness in them. Trust God to change your circumstances instead of putting up with them.

On one occasion my car went in for a service. The next morning I was due to leave on an important ministry trip, which I knew was in the centre of God's will. Late in the afternoon I rang the garage to see if the car was ready for collection, but, they told me 'No, we've found something wrong with it. It needs a spare part which we don't have and we can't get it until tomorrow, at the earliest.' After discovering what was wrong I said, 'If I can get the part, can you fit it so that I can leave tomorrow?' to which they agreed, although they insisted the part was unobtainable. First of all I called out to God, 'Help,' and then phoned the next nearest dealer of my car, which was about 50 miles away. They had got the part we needed and so one of my team drove up, and collected it. As soon as the garage opened, next morning, they fitted it and off I went. I could have taken the circumstances as saying that it was not God's will for me to go on this trip, but I knew it was and so I was not going to accept a 'No.' Nothing, and no one can keep me back when I know God's will for my life.

God can speak to us through circumstances, so we need to discern very clearly what is happening. If the situation is coming against you and God's will, then you must break through. You have got enough faith to change every circumstance this world could produce.

So in making big decisions, take these simple steps:

Step 1: Slow down, don't be in a rush.

Step 2: Pray, get the information from the right source.

Step 3: Be safe, check it out.

Step 4: Get moving!

In the next chapter, we will go on to look at the three ways God often uses to guide our steps.

Chapter 5

The Three Witnesses

We have seen that guidance is all about hearing God, and as we learn to recognise His voice we can be confident that we know His will for our lives. That is what Jesus meant when he said to His disciples, *'My sheep hear My voice, and I know them, and they follow Me.'* (John 10:27). When it comes to taking decisions, ones that are going to have a big effect on our lives, it is important to know without any doubt what God is saying. How can we be sure? There is a principle, a rule of thumb, which I use in these situations; it is found in Ecclesiastes 4:12.

> *'Though one may be overpowered by another, two can withstand him. And a threefold cord is not quickly broken.'*
>
> (Ecclesiastes 4:12)

When I need to make an important decision I ask the Lord for three clear witnesses. This does not happen every time, so please do not read this chapter like that. However looking for these three witnesses usually means I can be confident that I understand God's will.

Witness One: *The Word of God*

When I need God to speak to me, the first place I go to is His written Word, the Bible. I ask Him to give me a portion of scripture, or a verse straight from Himself. Do you use the Bible in this way? Do you understand that God will speak to you in a clear way from His Word? If you don't, then begin to expect God to speak to you in this way as you read the Bible.

Now don't try and use it like a 'magic' book. What I mean by that is like the old joke about the man who needed guidance. He opened the Bible and put his finger down saying, 'God speak to me.' The verse read '[Judas] *went out and hanged himself.'* Deciding that this was not the word he needed, he turned over another page and put his finger down again, *'Go and do likewise.'* He said, 'Lord, this can't be right. Please give me a verse' and he opened his Bible again, put his finger on a verse and it read, *'What you are about to do, do quickly!'*

That is not the way God will guide, and in fact is quite dangerous, because the result could be anything but God's will. I believe that the safest way is to

listen as you read the Word in your daily 'devotions'.
Look at the example Jesus set us. When He was
tempted in the wilderness, Satan came to Him three
times, and each time Jesus used scripture to answer
him. The verses He used all come from two chapters
in Deuteronomy (6 and 8). It is possible Jesus had
spent time meditating on those verses that day, as He
spent time talking with God.

Have you ever considered the idea that Jesus used
to read the Word regularly and have a time of 'personal devotions' or a 'Quiet time?' If you have problems in this area of self-discipline, ask Him to help
you. He was tempted in the same ways we are and I
am sure that on some mornings His flesh complained
about spending time with God, just like ours does.
Ask Jesus for help; He's been there before us!

Don't try to get guidance by the 'stick a pin in and
pull out a promise' method. That is the reason why I
do not recommend 'Promise Boxes.' It is possible
that God might use one in an exceptional circumstance, but as there are usually only good promises in
those boxes, I don't recommend them.

Witness Two: *An independent 'Amen'*

What do I mean by an independent 'Amen?' After
getting a word that is pointing the way ahead, I look
for someone who knows nothing at all about what I
need from God, to confirm the Word. A very good
example of this happened before I married Heather.
No one even knew that we were interested in each

other, and we had just begun to seek the Lord, saying 'Lord, speak to us.' Someone who lived in Jersey, in the Channel Islands, who I had met, but knew absolutely nothing about the situation, wrote me a letter. When I opened it, out fell a sprig of heather! In the letter, the person said 'I don't know why I'm sending you this piece of heather, but the Lord told me to put it in the envelope. I don't usually do this sort of thing, but here it is.' You can imagine what it said to me.

Later I told Heather's mother what had happened and showed the heather to her. She said, 'That is the identical type of heather that I picked when I was in Scotland after I had become pregnant. I felt that was the name I should call her. There are several different types of heather, but this is identical to what I picked.' For me that was an added confirmation to my independent witness.

Be aware that when you need guidance on a big, life-changing issue, God can move heaven and earth to confirm things in a way that you can hear and receive.

Witness Three: *A confirmation*

The last strand of the threefold cord I look for is the Lord's confirmation, putting His seal on what I have already heard. You could say that the confirmation and the independent 'Amen' appear to be the same thing. Sometimes they are, but I still like three, because that threefold cord cannot easily be broken.

One very important lesson to learn is that when you are looking to God for confirmation, it is possible that the gift of prophecy could be used. I have not mentioned it before because prophecy should only be used to **confirm** something that you have already been guided on. It is very unusual that God will begin to guide someone through the gift of prophecy.

I know of people who have had somebody lay hands on them, and for instance say, 'Thus saith the Lord, go to China.' The truth is that they have never had a burden or an interest in China or anything like that. If that type of 'word' is spoken to you, don't act on that prophecy. But if God has been speaking to you about working for Him in Italy, and you have had a word from Him, and an independent witness, when someone says something like, 'Thus saith the Lord, I would have you go to Italy,' accept that as God confirming what you have already heard. My advice is do not use prophecy as guidance in the first instance.

This is a scriptural approach, I believe, because the Bible says the gift of prophecy is for edification, exhortation and comfort (1 Corinthians 14:3). It saddens me to think of the many people, often youngsters, that I have met and prayed with whose lives have been shipwrecked because they hung all their life-decisions on a prophecy. Please, I beg of you do not allow prophecy to become the initiating guidance in your life. Let it only be a very definite confirmation.

Confirmation of God's leading can come in many different guises. It does not have to be a prophetic word. On one occasion confirmation came to me in the shape of three 10 dollar notes:

I was planning to go to the USA for the first time. We had sought God and He gave us very clear guidance that it was right to go. The tickets were booked, God provided the money to go and everything was fine. We had planned on a trip of about six weeks, with the first two weeks in a church in Chicago, and then we were believing the Lord to open up the rest from those two weeks of ministry. Three days before we were due to fly, I received a telegram saying the meetings were cancelled.

The moment we got that telegram both I and the brother who was travelling with me had a strong witness that the Lord was saying, 'Still go.' So, we said, 'Lord, do something, show us clearly what you want.' In the very next post a letter arrived and in it was 30 dollars and a note, 'The Lord has told me to send you this because you will need it when you are in America.' That was the confirmation I needed. If somebody had sent me a £100 cheque in sterling, or in Japanese yen or in any other currency, it would not have meant the same thing; but it came in American dollars as God's confirmation that our trip was right.

So there are the three strands of the cord:

1. The Word of God.
2. An independent 'Amen.'
3. A confirmation.

Look for those three when you are asking for guidance and you can be confident that you will hear what God is saying to you. When you act on that guidance, things may appear to go wrong but do not be shaken because your strong rope will hold you through the storm.

Are You Being Fleeced?

There is one area where many Christians get confused that I want to look at, and it is the use of 'fleeces.' I have deliberately not mentioned them above because they can be unhelpful when looking for confirmation. I think that the Church needs correcting about using fleeces. In Judges 6 we read:

> *'Then Gideon said to God, "If You will save Israel by my hand as You have said; look, I shall put a fleece of wool on the threshing floor; if there is dew on the fleece only, and it is dry on all the ground, then I shall know that You will save Israel by my hand, as You have said." And it was so. When he rose early the next morning and squeezed the fleece together, he wrung the dew out of the fleece, a bowl full of water. Then Gideon said to God, "Do not be angry with me, and let me speak just once more: Let me test, I pray, just once more with the fleece; let it now be dry only on the fleece, but on all the ground let there be dew." And God did so that night. It was dry on the fleece only, but there was dew on all the ground.'* (Judges 6:36–40)

The Bible gives us at least 4,000 years of history, and only once in all that time is a fleece used, in the passage you have just read. Once in over 4,000 years puts its use in context; what concerns me is that there are some Christians putting out two or three fleeces a day! I believe that using a fleece should be the exception and not the rule. Perhaps in a real crisis, if it comes to the crunch you might need to use a fleece, but keep it balance. Do not live by fleeces; we don't need them, if we really trust the Lord.

I had a friend, a lovely Christian who was really serving the Lord in a wonderful way, who got fed up with his job and wanted a new one. He prayed about it, but didn't get much response from heaven so decided to try putting out a fleece. When he went to bed he said, 'Lord, if the light bulb comes on in the morning, I'll know you want me to leave my job, but if it fuses in the night and does not work when I switch it on, I know you want me to stay where I am.' In the morning, he got up and switched the light on and of course the bulb lit. On the basis of that he went to work and gave his notice in.

That happened several years ago and since then his family has had nothing but trouble. Sadder still, my friend has backslidden and gone away from God. What happened? He misused the fleece; you see, if God has not told you to change your employment, stay where you are. It is important to accept that the initiative for change should be with God, not with you. My friend took the initiative and got lost. That is what concerns me about using fleeces; too often they are used by people who are taking the initiative, instead of letting God lead.

Before you discard the idea of fleeces entirely, let me give you a personal testimony. I was in a quandary; Heather and I were at a conference which was lasting two weeks. We had enough money to pay for the first week and then we intended to go home, but while we were there it seemed that the Lord wanted us to stay for the second week. So Heather and I put out a fleece. We prayed, 'Lord, if you provide the money for us to stay the second week then we'll stay.' No one knew what we had prayed, but shortly afterwards we found an envelope pushed under the door of our room. In it was enough money to pay the conference fees for the second week.

That was wonderful, our fleece had been answered, but Heather and I were unsure. There were other things we could use the money for back at home. What should we do? So, we went back to the Lord, and said 'Lord, do you really want us to stay here next week?' putting the fleece out a second time.

The conference was being run by a dear brother, Edgar Trout; Edgar was very sensitive to the Holy Spirit. That meant you could not afford to play with God, because God often used Edgar to expose anything that was hidden. In the next meeting after we had prayed the second time, somebody had a vision of a fleece. The fleece was on two sticks, tied with two ropes and it was being stretched. I did not apply it to myself until Edgar brought the interpretation of the picture. He said, 'Somebody here has put a fleece out to the Lord, and now they have put out another one. What they are trying to do is stretch the fleece.' I stood up and accepted that God had already told us what His will was and we did not need to check it again.

So, please use fleeces sparingly. God will make His will known to you, if you approach Him in faith. Look for the three strands of the cord and you can have confidence that the will of God will be done on earth as it is done in heaven.

Guidance
and the
Call of God

Chapter 6

God's Work of Art

As Christians it is essential that we know what we are supposed to be doing. Too often people live aimless lives, without goals, dreams or visions. They aim at nothing and score a bull's-eye, every time! If you have no idea what you are supposed to be doing for God, then this chapter is for you.

The most important thing in my life is the will of God. To live in the centre of God's will should be the most important thing in every person's life. As I live there, I have everything I will ever need; I am in complete safety and security, and I will know God's provision. *'Not everyone who says to Me, "Lord, Lord," shall enter the kingdom of heaven, but he who does the will of My Father in heaven.'* (Matthew 7:21). It is not just knowing Jesus that gets us into the kingdom, but it is doing the will of God. I believe everyone has a specific call from God; He has a blueprint for the lives of each one of His children.

Perfectly Made for the Job

'Know that the LORD, He is God; It is He who has made us, and not we ourselves.'

(Psalm 100:3)

That is tremendous! God made us; we didn't come from a lump of jelly, God created something special when He made us. Ephesians 2:10 says *'For we are His workmanship, created in Christ Jesus for good works.'* The Jerusalem Bible says *'We are His work of art.'* I find that thrilling: I am God's work of art! Think about the craftsman who made us. Are there any flaws or mistakes in His work? Of course not, I'm His work of art, so I'm just right.

I meet so many people who spend most of their lives wishing they were somebody else, or wanting to do something else, to live elsewhere, to do a different job to the one they have got. These people are sure that they would be much happier if they could just change their situation. The truth is that if they could get the change they wanted, within a very short time they would be wishing for another change. One of the great freedoms in the world is to recognise that God made us, that we are His work of art and to accept that as fact. I am thrilled to be Don Double! I'm just right – 6′ 5½″ tall, with blue eyes, etc.; God made me and so I enjoy being Don Double every day. It is wonderful just to be who He has made me to be and there is great fulfilment in following the blueprint that God designed for me day by day.

If you don't feel the same thrill about being you, turn to God. Ask Him to show you what He feels about you. Accept that you are just right because He made you, and that He made you for some special 'good works.' Then take a very important step, decide to enjoy the way God made you and praise Him every day.

Circles or Straight Lines?

Many people spend much of their life going around in circles. What do I mean? They live like the children of Israel who took forty years to get from the Red Sea to the Promised Land; a journey which should have taken eleven days. Why did they take so long? They spent forty years in the desert going round in circles! It took them that long to learn what God needed to teach them. They needed to be prepared for the Promised Land, but it took a long time, making the same mistakes over and over again, before they were ready to go in.

There is one thing you need to know about going round in circles – you always come back to the same place! You can't avoid it. For many people the drudge of going around in a circle, never achieving anything, can be described as a 'vicious circle.' If that describes you, be encouraged – God is in the business of breaking vicious circles. He can release you from it and give you a vision of what He wants to do through your life.

Square Pegs in Round Holes

It may be that you know that God has called you, but you are still frustrated and feel bound in what you do. God's word to you is, if He has called you to be a 'square peg', don't try to live in a 'round hole'. For instance, if God has called you to be an evangelist and you are trying to do the job of a pastor, you are a square peg in a round hole.

I know of a church with a congregation of about one thousand people; it's a wonderful church as far as it goes. The 'pastor' was an evangelist who spent thirty years caring for the church. The reason why the church was so big was because he just kept winning souls to Jesus. Now, there is nothing wrong with winning people to the Lord, but those Christians remained spiritual babies, shallow and immature. Why? That man had no ability to take them in any deeper into the things of God; he just kept on evangelising and winning souls and seeing the church grow numerically. That was great, but how much more wonderful it would have been, if there had been a pastor in the church to teach the flock and to build them up. That man could have been released to more evangelism, knowing the church was cared for.

You may not be an evangelist or a pastor, but whatever God has called you to, make sure you are in the right place. Be real about what God has called you to do. I remember a man who came to preach on a Sunday night at my home church in Cornwall. He was a student in Bible school and the truth was that, after he had ministered, we went home feeling worse than when we went in!

I had the job of taking him back to where he was staying after the meeting, and as we drove I asked him, 'Brother, tell me about your call.' He replied, 'Oh, I haven't had one of them.' That was obvious, and if he had been called, it certainly was not to preach. That man went through Bible School, and has since pastored several churches, and everyone of them has flopped and been a failure. Here is a man in the ministry without a call from God, and it has been sad to watch, both for the man and for the people that have been damaged along the way.

> *'But now God has set the members, each one of them, in the body just as He pleased.'*
>
> (1 Corinthians 12:18)

One of the most liberating things a Christian can discover is the place God has prepared for them in His Body, the Church. As we have already seen many people try to fit in places that God didn't intend them to be. The result is frustration because they are like the proverbial square peg. It is even sadder to realise that not only will those people be frustrated but also the people who are in the right place around them that need a 'round peg;' they can't function to their full potential. Then there are the people who are waiting for a square peg to fill the hole in their lives, and also there is also the 'round peg' whose place is being filled. We are dealing with an important issue, and as I visit churches all over this country I see this happening on too many occasions.

As you look around your church or fellowship can you identify the people who are in the wrong place? It may be that you are one of them; think about the implications of the right person not doing their God ordained job. Somebody else will probably be trying to do the job, as well as doing their own. At least two sets of people are likely to be missing God's best, because there is never enough time to do a proper job. We are considering an issue that could revolutionise your church if all its members started to do the jobs God has called them to do (and I'm positive your leaders would be extremely blessed as well.)

Jesus said He would build His Church (Matthew 16:18) and if we allow Him to place us in the Body, being obedient to His calling, we will find ourselves in the right place. Each of us needs to know that we have been placed by God into His Body; He has prepared a place just for us, and when we are in it we need to commit ourselves to fully function, serving faithfully and reliably.

In 1 Corinthians 12 Paul writes a very detailed account about how the body works. He starts by saying that everyone is different but needs each other:

> *'The body is one and has many members, but all the members of that one body, being many, are one body.'*

(verse 12)

60

'For in fact the body is not one member but many. If the foot should say, "Because I am not a hand, I am not of the body," is it therefore not of the body? And if the ear should say, "Because I am not an eye, I am not of the body," is it therefore not of the body? If the whole body were an eye, where would be the hearing? If the whole were hearing, where would be the smelling?'

(verses 14–17)

He goes on to make clear that we cannot separate ourselves from the rest of the body:

'And the eye cannot say to the hand, "I have no need of you"; nor again the head to the feet, "I have no need of you." No, much rather, those members of the body which seem to be weaker are necessary. And those members of the body which we think to be less honourable, on these we bestow greater honour; and our unpresentable parts have greater modesty.'

(verses 21–23)

'that there should be no schism in the body, but that the members should have the same care for one another.'

(verse 25)

Paul then goes on to list some of the parts of the body including apostles, prophets and teachers (verse 28), but I want to draw your attention to other roles that are just as vital to the life and growth of the

Body. Paul mentions the gifts of helps and administrations. This speaks to me of ministries that happen 'behind the scenes,' they are not done by people standing in front of a large crowd. Often those who help and administrate are out of sight and so get forgotten or ignored. Those who put the chairs out, visit the lonely, transport people to meetings, make it their job to ensure the toilets are working, all those are 'spiritual' ministries if done for the Lord.

No one is called just to sit on a chair (or pew) and keep it warm! Everyone is called to be a functioning member of the Body of Christ.

> *'Christ, from whom the whole body, joined and knit together by what every joint supplies, according to the effective working by which every part does its share, causes growth of the body for the edifying of itself in love.'*
>
> (Ephesians 4:16)

One final comment about the Body and your relationship to it: If you are not a committed, functioning part of a local expression of the Body of Christ, do something about it quickly. You need to be belong to a church and they need you. Too many people have convinced themselves that they are OK not belonging to a church – that is a deception of Satan, that is robbing both those people and the church who urgently need their gifts and ministries.

In the next chapter we will look at what being called entails, but before you read on, spend some time talking to God about your calling. Do you know that you are called? If you don't, reach out in faith and listen to what He has to say. Are you a square peg? If you feel you are, talk to your Father about it and begin to believe and receive a square hole!

Chapter 7

An Expensive Calling

'Then the word of the LORD came to me, saying: "Before I formed you in the womb I knew you; before you were born I sanctified you; and I ordained you a prophet to the nations." Then said I: "Ah, Lord GOD! Behold, I cannot speak, for I am a youth." But the LORD said to me: "Do not say, 'I am a youth,' for you shall go to all to whom I send you, and whatever I command you, you shall speak. Do not be afraid of their faces, for I am with you to deliver you," says the LORD. Then the LORD put forth His hand and touched my mouth, and the LORD said to me: "Behold, I have put My words in your mouth. See, I have this day set you over the nations and over the kingdoms, to root out and to pull down, to destroy and to throw down, to build and to plant."'

(Jeremiah 1:4–10)

God has a specific call for every person and we need to know what that calling is. Look at Jeremiah's call in the passage above.

When the Going Gets Tough

'The word of the LORD came to me, saying.' (verse 4). It's good to know where the call comes from. Some people tell me that their church has called them or that it has come from some other source. Jeremiah's call came direct from God, and I believe God will do the same for you. When you know God's word has come to you, you can go through anything, whatever the cost. If you are hanging onto the words of a man, when the storm comes you are likely to drown. When you have God's word, you can hang onto something that will get you through.

'But the LORD said to me: "Do not say, 'I am a youth,' for you shall go to all to whom I send you, and whatever I command you, you shall speak. Do not be afraid of their faces, for I am with you to deliver you," *says the LORD.'* (verses 7–8). What a promise to go with. When God calls don't say, 'I can't do it.' If God calls you to do something, He will give you the ability to do that job. It is that simple, you can do it. Paul proved that and wrote, *'I can do all things through Christ who strengthens me.'* (Philippians 4:13).

When you know what God has called you to do, it becomes the driving force to keep going when things get tough. God has not promised we will have an easy life. I have had a few tough times in my life, but I have known the call of God and it's kept me going.

On one occasion I can remember lying in a mud hut in Kenya, way out in the bush. It was a typical African mud hut and because I was an honoured guest they had freshly cow-dunged the floor. The missionaries I was working with had been very kind and had provided a camp bed for me, so that I did not have to sleep on the floor. The bed was the type that you can roll up and almost carry in your pocket; put together they are two feet wide and six foot long. I am 6' 5½" tall and normally when I get into a 6' bed, I just pull my knees up to get comfortable. This bed was 2' wide and so I couldn't even get my knees up. There were rats running around the floor, and poisonous spiders on the walls and so I laid there for a long time, debating whether it was safest to put my feet over the bottom of the bed or my head over the top. It was well into the early hours of the morning before I went to sleep!

As I lay there I had to ask myself, 'What am I doing here?' I could easily drive to Nairobi the next day, get on a plane and fly home to my wife and children, and to a nice comfortable bed. There was nothing in this world to stop me doing that, except the call of God. I knew I was called of God to be there, and because of that call, I came to the place where it was a joy to be there, even in those adverse circumstances. Nothing can rob you of the joy of the Lord, if you know that God has called you to be in a specific place at a specific time.

> *'If any of you lacks wisdom, let him ask of God, who gives to all liberally and without reproach, and it will be given to him. But let him ask in faith, with no doubting, for he who doubts is like a wave of the sea driven and tossed by the wind. For let not that man suppose that he will receive anything from the Lord; he is a double-minded man, unstable in all his ways.'*
>
> (James 1:5–8)

If you are double-minded about your call, 'in two-minds' about what you are supposed to be doing, you will be unstable. When the wind of adverse circumstances blow against you, what happens? Those doubts produce, 'Am I supposed to be doing this?' 'Should I be here? 'Is this right? Everything seems to be going wrong.' Even if circumstances appear to be going wrong, your call will get you through. However, if you are double-minded, instability is the result, which often makes the situation worse.

Fulfilling Our Potential

God told Jeremiah not argue with Him, (verses 7–8). Too many of us spend our lives arguing with God, usually because we don't see things from His perspective. We are too tied up with our problems, and say like Jeremiah, *'Ah, Lord GOD! Behold, I cannot speak, for I am a youth.'* We miss the truth that God sees beyond what we are now, to what He will make us to be.

When God called me I couldn't read, write or spell. I could just about manage to write my own name, and read a few words with a real struggle; the reason for this was that I missed much of my schooling because I had tuberculosis twice as a young man. At the age of 20, when I was saved, I was working on a farm digging ditches. The moment I was saved God began to lift me. That's what God will do for you, Hallelujah! The reality is that faith in the living Jesus, is different from just being religious, because in believing in Him, God will lift you. He wants to prosper us and for us to make progress. So many people have got the concept that God wants to crush us and keep us down, but that is a lie.

Abraham was called the friend of God and look how God blessed him. I'm God's friend too (John 15:15) and I am convinced that He's going to bless me in the same way. You need to make that your confession. God can really do things, if you believe Him. The blessing of God came to Abraham because he believed God (Romans 4:3).

After I was saved I met a Congregational minister who helped me greatly. I can remember going to him and saying, 'You keep talking about education. Can God give **me** an education?' He very wisely pointed me to the Scriptures, to Acts 4:13:

'Now when they saw the boldness of Peter and John, and perceived that they were uneducated and untrained men, they marvelled.'

That was me, uneducated and untrained, but the minister went on to show me that when they were filled with the Holy Spirit, Peter and John were among those who *'turned the world upside down'* (Acts 17:6). He told me that if I got baptized in the Holy Spirit, and I wanted it for His glory, God would give me all the education I needed. Through the baptism in the Holy Spirit all I have today came from Him. I did not get it from any earthly source. Heather, my very patient wife, will testify to that. She has tried very hard on some occasions to teach me things, but somehow I have not been able to comprehend what she was saying. Through the power of the Holy Spirit, God has provided for me.

When God called me it was very specific. On the day after I was baptised in the Holy Spirit, I was kneeling in my lounge, speaking in tongues for the second time in my life. The voice of God spoke very clearly to me; I don't know whether it was an audible voice or not, but I knew it was God speaking to me. He said 'I call you to be an Evangelist; an Evangelist to the villages and small towns.' Since that day I have seen God fulfil that call in many ways.

From that day on, I have sought to live in obedience to that call, and at various times God has used people to bring further direction. One word said, 'You shall preach to nations, you shall preach on television, you shall preach on the radio.' Another said, 'You shall stand before leaders of nations and before important people and speak my word.' Now I could have responded like Jeremiah and say I'm just a poor little back-street fellow who is struggling to make a living, and wouldn't say boo to a goose!' But, I didn't; I accepted them as the word of God, and every word has come true. God has not failed one word of what He said He would do.

With the call came the ability to do those things. Sometimes I have been preaching, and in the same way that you would speak in tongues, I have spoken in English. I have spoken words I did not know the meaning of, but God gave me the words to speak and I spoke them. Afterwards, members of my team have said that my words meant exactly what God wanted to express. He can do it, and I want to encourage you to believe that there is no limitation on God when you abide in His call, whatever that call is.

Counting the Cost

In Luke 5 we read of Jesus calling Peter. What was Peter's reaction? Verse 8 says that when he saw Jesus demonstrate the Holy Spirit's power *'he fell down at Jesus' knees, saying, "Depart from me, for I am a sinful man, O Lord!"'* He was saying, 'Lord get out of my way, you worry me being around here.' Jesus turned round to him and said, *'Do not be afraid. From now on you will catch men.'* There is nothing to be afraid of when God calls you, nothing at all. You can't see into the future, and you don't know how it is all going to work out but if He's called you, that should be good enough for you.

71

When Peter received the call, he believed the word and Luke 5:11 says he, *'forsook all and followed Him.'* In other words Peter made a total commitment, which is what the call of God always demands. You cannot serve two masters (Matthew 6:24) and the call of God will demand every part of your being, your time, your talents, your family, everything.

A friend of mine tells of an incident that happened to her that illustrates the choice we face. She was preaching in a big church; hundreds of people were there and it had been a tremendous meeting, many had been saved, healed, filled with the Spirit and blessed. At the meeting's close, she was walking back to the room where she had left her coat, when she met a lady that she had not seen for over 20 years. The two of them had shared a room at Bible School, but had not seen each other since. After greeting each other, they began to talk about their lives since college. The other lady said, 'I've had a sad life. I got married and then divorced, I've been right away from God and everything has gone wrong. I'm totally broken and there's nothing but misery in my life.' Then she said 'I would have given anything to have been in your shoes tonight.' My friend replied, 'That is exactly what it cost me, everything.'

In responding to the call you must count the cost. It will demand total commitment. God is the one who calls and He is the one who enables, if we are prepared to give up everything. I have shared from my personal experience in the hope that you begin to understand what being called means. You may not be called as an Evangelist; in fact, as we will see in the next chapter, the Lord has a great variety of jobs to do in His kingdom. However, the cost is the same for everyone and you will never fulfil your calling without a total commitment to it.

Chapter 8

Called to Serve

As we have already seen God has a job for each one of us to do. He has created us for work: *'For we are His workmanship, created in Christ Jesus for good works, which God prepared beforehand that we should walk in them.'* (Ephesians 2:10). When Jeremiah was called by God, he too received a specific job:

> *'Before I formed you in the womb I knew you; before you were born I sanctified you; and I ordained you a prophet to the nations.'*
>
> (Jeremiah 1:5)

> *'Then the LORD put forth His hand and touched my mouth, and the LORD said to me: "Behold, I have put My words in your mouth. See, I have this day set you over the nations and over the*

kingdoms, to root out and to pull down, to destroy and to throw down, to build and to plant."'

(Jeremiah 1:9–10)

Before the Lord started to make Jeremiah in his mother's womb, He knew him. Isn't that a wonderful thought? Almighty God sanctified Jeremiah, He had set him apart and chosen him before he was born. Are you aware that God knows all there is to know about you? So often we forget that important truth – God knows and He cares.

Jeremiah was called to be a prophet, a man with God's words in his mouth. Note that the call was very specific, he was a prophet to the nations. The Lord laid down the boundaries of his activity and so the prophet was to expect to speak to all the nations. My prayer is that God would call men to the same job today. We need prophets who will speak to the nations at the end of the Twentieth century. Prophecy is not just for people who sit in cosy churches; it should be the authoritative voice of God speaking to our national leaders and decision makers.

For many years I have been praying that God will raise up a prophet in Parliament. That is where the voice of God needs to be heard; how tremendous it would be if God called a man and elected him to Parliament to declare His Word. Are you prepared to accept such a clear call from God?

It is not just within politics that God's voice needs to be declared. I have been preaching for a long time that God calls people to be school teachers. One of the greatest needs in this country is for our schools to be filled with Christian school teachers. Whilst we are inactive, the devil is working and men and women who are humanists, communists, and even New Agers are taking key teaching posts. We need to pray for Christians to hear God's call into our schools. For me, being called to be a school teacher is just as significant as being called to be an Apostle or Evangelist.

God called one young lady to be teacher, during one of our Teens and Twenties weekends. She went to college and got her qualifications but then couldn't get a job. Every job she tried for had hundreds of applicants, and because she had no experience, there was no chance of her getting the post. She came to me in despair, doubting that God had called her. I encouraged her to believe with me that God was going to get her a job. And He did! She came to me during the summer holidays, two or three weeks before the start of term. At that point there were no vacancies to apply for, but as we prayed she found one. There were over four hundred applicants for that job, but two days before the beginning of term, she was given the job, and she is still in it today. God had called her; He is faithful and will work it out for you too.

On one occasion I was ministering in the USA and met the Mayor of Charlestown, Indiana. He is a tremendous man of God, and he told me how he became Mayor. The town was in a dreadful mess; it was bankrupt, its prisons were full, crime was on the increase, and the people of the town did not know what to do. A group of men were praying about the situation, and one day God spoke to them. He told them that the way out was to get a Christian Mayor. So they said, 'OK, who do we get, Lord?' He showed them a man, and they went to him and said, 'The Lord has chosen you to be Mayor!' Somewhat surprised he responded 'How can I be Mayor? I'm too shy, I'm not political and nobody knows me.' All the men could say was that they knew that God had called him to be Mayor.

He prayed about it, felt it was right and so when the election came they nominated him, and of course he won. Straight away he began to preach the gospel from his position as Mayor. He went into the prisons and preached the gospel to the prisoners. Most of them got saved, and those that didn't told the other criminals in the area, 'Don't commit any crimes in this town, because if you get caught and thrown in jail, they will preach at you!' When I was there I think there was only one prisoner in the entire jail – God had emptied the prison! That alone helped the town's finances, but the Mayor prayed about the large debt they owed and very soon God had so blessed them that the debt was cleared. This man accepted God's call on his life and was prepared to let God use him, the result was an entire community was changed.

God can call you. You may be a potential city councillor, are you willing to hear God's call? I am sure God wants to call people into the leadership of major organisations like the trade unions. Don't sit back, seek the Lord about it. Think of the impact upon this country if the President of the mine workers, or the steel workers or the car makers was a Spirit-filled Christian. The impact they could have on the nation is enormous.

Another area which desperately needs the influence of Christian men and women is journalism and the media. We need national newspaper editors, TV directors, producers and administrators, and writers who love God and are prepared to work in these key jobs. God could be calling you, it will take hard work to get there, but are you prepared to follow where God leads?

I meet many people around this country who have been called into business by God. If that is your calling, know that He calls you to be a successful businessman or woman. I know a man who God called into business. He had no money, so he went down to the bank and borrowed some. He promptly gave it away and said, 'Lord, I've paid my tithe; now you have to provide the money for what you've called me to do,' and the Lord did. He was given a run down petrol station, that was ready to be scrapped. I have bought petrol from there since, and it is like going to church! The presence of God is all round that place. All the workers are Christians and hand out tracts to the people who come to fill their cars with petrol. I have stood on that courtyard and seen cars queuing up for petrol. On the other side of the road is another petrol station, owned by one of the big chains, and occasionally a car goes in there; but, at this one they are pumping petrol as fast as they can go all the time, because it's God's petrol station.

After that station was running well, my friend bought another one, and today he's got at least three, all doing very well because God called him to be a businessman. When he started he gave a tenth, his tithe to the Lord; today, he gives nine tenths of all he earns to the Lord and lives on a tenth, and lives well, because God called him. You will read in the Bible of the ministry of giving. I believe today that this is the ministry of the God-called businessman or woman. The Church needs vast resources to do its job properly, to send people out into the harvest fields of the world; one way in which God provides is through the businessmen and women He has called to be successful.

It may be that as you have read this section you have felt that none of those things applied to you and that God has not got such 'grand' things for you to do. God may not be calling you into such positions of power, but pray for the people God is calling, they need your support in prayer.

> *'Whatever you do in word or deed, do all in the name of the Lord Jesus, giving thanks to God the Father through Him.'*

(Colossians 3:17)

If you approach your job with that attitude, believing that God has placed you in it for His purpose and according to His will, then do not worry about missing God's will. The kingdom of God is bigger than we can imagine, and there are many different jobs to be done. The most important job is not to become an apostle or an evangelist or a vicar, it is to be obedient to what God has called you to do. Therefore you can mend roads for the council, fill shelves at the supermarket, or look after people's money in the bank, and do it all for Jesus. 'Full time service' in the kingdom is not about who pays your wages, it is to do with your attitude to God and the work you do.

The Language of Faith

I hope that you are beginning to get excited about the call God has on your life. Begin to pray and believe that you will hear clearly when He calls. However, before we go on it is important to recognise the lesson in verse 10 of Jeremiah 1:

'See, I have this day set you over the nations and over the kingdoms, to root out and to pull down, to destroy and to throw down, to build and to plant.'

(Jeremiah 1:10)

You may ask 'what's significant about that verse?' It is the word you most probably overlooked as you read the verse. God said to Jeremiah, *'See ... '*

Brother, sister, it is no good going out blindly. When you are called, don't step out in 'blind faith,' wait for God to show you what you have to do. People talk about 'blind faith,' but there is nothing blind about faith. Real faith is full of life, and if you are full of life, you can see.

> *'Now faith is the substance of things hoped for, the evidence of things not seen.'*
>
> (Hebrews 11:1)

If you have heard the call of God, but have no faith, you will never fulfil the call, because it can only be fulfilled in faith. When God spoke, Jeremiah had no evidence at all, but the Lord said, 'See ... have a good look.'

God said it was happening *'this day.'* Not some day in the future, it was happening then. God always speaks in the language of faith; remember that when God talks to you, He talks to you in words of faith. To Jeremiah He said, 'No one has ever heard of you Jeremiah, but I know who you are. Today, I have taken you and I have placed you over the nations and kingdoms; that's where you are already.' What God was doing was giving Jeremiah the authority he needed to fulfil his call. It is important that you recognise that with the call of God comes the authority to do the job.

When you begin to fulfil the call of God, you move in the authority of God. He has given it to you and there is not a demon in hell who can stand against that authority. There is not a man on the earth who can close the door to my God. If God says 'Go, and you shall stand before kings and princes,' you will stand before them. If God says 'Go to China and preach to the Chinese Government,' there is not one single Communist who can stop you doing it. Once you have got the word of the Lord, He sets you in a position of authority to do it.

A young man, who used to be a member of my team, was called to be a school teacher for a while. He got a job in one of the London schools where it was very unruly and there was no discipline at all. It was a regular occurrence for teachers to be taken into hospital with nervous breakdowns because of the heavy pressure of teaching in that school. This young man went confident that God had called him to do this job. Some of the children were bigger than him, but he knew he had God's authority to do the job.

He went into those classrooms and simply believed the authority God had given him. Amazingly, in a class of children, who were normally rowdy and rebellious, nobody spoke a word, and everyone behaved perfectly. It soon got around the school that this man had complete authority in his classroom. Eventually, when he had a free period the other teachers would invite him to just go and sit in their classroom while they taught. There would not be a murmur, and it continued until the day he left the school, and entered full time Christian ministry for the Lord.

When God calls us He gives us all the authority we need to fulfil His will in our lives. If He has set us over the situation, we are already in a superior state, and you need to believe it. Whatever God has called you to do, He's given you the authority to do it.

This authority does not work only when you are in a 'ministry' or work situation. Those of you who have children, have been called to be parents and you have God's authority to fulfil that role. If we don't demonstrate the call of God to be parents in our homes, we will never demonstrate it in the church, or anywhere else. You need to recognise the authority God has given you. When you speak, the whole of heaven is behind what you say, if you believe it. Make sure your children recognise the authority of God in your lives as parents.

You have an excellent opportunity to demonstrate the authority of God in your home. All around you families are breaking up; the divorce statistics continue to rise at an alarming rate. The reality is that people want to know how to make the family work. It's the biggest problem there is today, and we have a precious opportunity to show the love of God in our family lives, as our children grow up in the fear and the admonition of the Lord.

Doing what God has called you to do, is the most fulfilling and rewarding work in the world. What is more worthwhile than contributing to the establishment and growth of something which is going to last forever? Please don't get the idea that because you enjoy serving God, that what you are doing is wrong.

I meet too many Christians who think that if they enjoy God's call on their life, it must be their flesh in control. The best things in life, the things that I enjoy doing most, are those that come from God, and in fact if I begin to not enjoy my daily walk and work, that is the time I have to ask God if I have missed His guidance. The Christian life is to be enjoyed to the full because God is good and all things that come from Him are good.

We have reached the end of this book, and my prayer is that you have learnt how simple the issue of guidance can be. Whether it is for big decisions or normal, everyday living God is interested. He wants you to stay in His will, because there He can bless you. If you want that, then you have come into agreement with God; remember that

'I am persuaded that neither death nor life, nor angels nor principalities nor powers, nor things present nor things to come, nor height nor depth, nor any other created thing, shall be able to separate us from the love of God which is in Christ Jesus our Lord.'

(Romans 8:38–39)

Appendix

A Study in Acts

Throughout the book of Acts we see the early Church getting established; it is an interesting project to look at how God guided those early Christians. As you study the lives of the real people who fill the pages of Acts, notice the different ways in which they were guided. A lot of guidance was 'ordinary' for everyday life, but it produced extraordinary events. Some came in unusual ways to help them at important points in the Church's growth. As you read, begin to have faith that you will experience the same; practice the 'ordinary' guidance of daily life and believe that you too will get the extraordinary when you need it.

Do What You Have Been Told To Do

'He commanded them not to depart from Jerusalem, but to wait for the Promise of the

Father ... you shall be baptized with the Holy Spirit not many days from now.'

(Acts 1:4–5)

'And He said to them, "Go into all the world and preach the gospel to every creature."'

(Mark 16:15)

There are many things that you do not need a special word from heaven about. You already know what God has commanded; all you have to do is get on and do as you have been told. Throughout the book of Acts this truth can be seen repeatedly. The Apostles simply did what Jesus had instructed them to do. For instance, you do not need to be told to preach the gospel to every creature, because Jesus has already made His will known on that subject. The Lord Jesus said 'Go and do the job,' and so wherever you find a creature, preach the gospel to them.

Living in the Spirit

'So continuing daily with one accord in the temple, and breaking bread from house to house, they ate their food with gladness and simplicity of heart, praising God and having favor with all the people. And the Lord added to the church daily those who were being saved.'

(Acts 2:46–47, see also 5:42)

As the church went about their daily routine, they found things began to happen because they were automatically living in the Spirit. In your daily routine believe that God will use you. If you are in a shop and a shop assistant has a need, meet it; if someone you work with needs help, do something about it. To expect God to use you at the level of ordinary living does not need any special guidance and yet quite extraordinary things will happen.

Having looked at their normal lives let's look at some of the more unusual events they were involved in:

Angelic Guidance

God sent angels to the early Church to give them guidance on five occasions: Acts 5:19–20, 8:26, 10:3, 12:8 and 27:23–24.

God sent an angel to give them specific directions, and He can still do the same today. On one occasion God sent an angel to me to speak to me and it was guidance that I desperately needed.

Led by the Spirit

Seven times Luke, the author of Acts, simply speaks about being led by the Spirit or the Spirit speaking: Acts 8:29, 10:19, 11:28; 13:2–4, 13:9–10, 16:6–7, and 18:5.

As we have already discussed keeping our ears opened to what God has to say is one of the most important ways we will be guided.

Visions

On five occasions they received visions: Acts 9:10, 10:3, 10:10, 16:9–10, and 18:9.

It's quite remarkable how God used visions to open up new areas of ministry.

A Need

In Acts 8:14 the apostles simply heard of a need and they did something about it. That is very important; I think some people get bound up with hearing the 'right guidance' and they overlook the simple things. The apostles were told of a need, they were able to help and so they did.

The 'Macedonian Call'

> *'And a vision appeared to Paul in the night. A man of Macedonia stood and pleaded with him, saying, "Come over to Macedonia and help us." Now after he had seen the vision, immediately we sought to go to Macedonia, concluding that the Lord had called us to preach the gospel to them.'*
> (Acts 16:9–10)

Paul and his team were called to help, and so they went. In the type of ministry I am in, the same often happens for me. I regularly receive 'Macedonian calls' from different parts of the world to go and help the church gather in the harvest. Often it can be hard deciding which are really the ones God wants me to answer, but it is still a valid way of getting guidance. Be open for someone to call for help in this way.

Prophetic Direction

Acts 21:11 records that the prophet Agabus gave Paul some specific direction from God. Please understand there is a big difference between the gift of prophecy and the ministry of a prophet. We need Prophets today, in fact Paul says in Ephesians 4:11 that God has given them to the Church, so that we might be equipped for the things He wants us to do. (For a further study of the office of Prophet and the gift of Prophecy, and the differences between the two, read the relevant chapter in my book 'Life in a new dimension.')

Circumstances

In Acts 8:4–5 we see that circumstances in the form of persecution scattered the Church. It marked a new stage in the Church's life as many of the people in the Jerusalem church had to run for their lives. Often God will use events around us to get us into the place He needs us; for instance, many people have taken the plunge into full time ministry after being made redundant. God finished their job to get them working for Him. Don't be discouraged when circumstances force you to move or change aspects of your life; ask God what new opportunities He is opening up to you.

The Voice of God
When it happens, you will know it. In Acts 23:11 God spoke directly to Paul. That was an exciting privilege and I'm sure that if He speaks that clearly to you, you will feel the same.

Prayer
A lot happens while people are in prayer, and the early Church provides ample evidence of that: Acts 3:1, 6:6, 8:15, 9:40, 10:9, 12:12, 13:3, 16:16 & 25, and 28:8.

Prayer is all to do with listening to God and communicating with Him. As we pray God will give us the information we need, so that we can stay in the very centre of His will.

Do not get bogged down by 'God will guide me in this way', or 'God always guides me in that way.' Be open, God is a God who enjoys variety and He will use all kinds of ways to speak to us and lead us.

Also by Don Double
The Five Facts of Life

Don's best-selling introduction to faith in Jesus Christ. In this short, easy-to-read booklet Don sets out five basic facts every person needs to face concerning their relationship with God.

This booklet has been used by many people as a useful tool in winning friends to faith in Jesus. The booklet concludes with a challenge to face the facts and a prayer of commitment.

It has been translated and used with great fruitfulness in many countries, including Russia, Romania, Rwanda, Pakistan, Bulgaria, Kenya and Burundi.

Price 75p

By Don's wife, Heather Double
Twentieth Century Eve

Ever since Adam and Eve's fall, women have lived under the oppression of their monthly cycle. This regular period was created by God, but are the traumas of premenstrual tension part of the divine order? Heather directly addresses the realities of being a woman, as God designed her, and shows from the Bible, how women can live balanced, fulfilled and victorious lives.

Price £1.95

Do you need healing? Then try

Healing The JESUS Way

Jesus healed people. Even a quick reading of the Gospels reveals that Jesus spent a large part of his ministry caring for the individual needs of people. He healed them in a variety of ways, but He always healed those who came to Him. Whoever you are, whatever your condition, Jesus can heal you. *Healing The JESUS Way*, is a book that will encourage your faith and point you to The Healer – Jesus Christ.

Price £3.95

Healing Highlights

Throughout the book are a number of testimonies from people who have been healed through the ministry of Don Double and the Good News Crusade team. They have been included as evidence of what God is doing for people, TODAY. From Blodwen Jones in north Wales, who suffered from osteoarthritis for 69 years, to Elizabeth Nakanwagi in Uganda, who was raised from her death-bed, all the stories show what changes can happen when you meet Jesus the Healer.

From a St Austell doctor:

Dear Don,

I found your book very inspiring; when I had finished it I thought that it was the most rounded, whole book that I had read on healing because it brought us right to the only healer – Jesus.

I praise God for your book, I have recommended it to many others and keep it in the surgery to lend as well. As a G.P. I know so well in my heart that Jesus is our only healer.

Thank you

A.D. St Austell

Dear Mr Double,

I thought I would write and tell you of the experience I had after saying the prayer on page 26 of your book Healing The JESUS Way. *I was not really a Christian before, I tried in vain to find faith but to no avail. Then a Christian friend of mine lent me your book; on reading through it I reached page 26 and I thought 'Well, I have nothing to lose.' Being one to often suffer from bouts of depression I thought 'here goes' and being scared, I must admit I thought at first nothing would happen to me. For the first couple of days nothing did, then whilst I was asleep God spoke to me. He told me to turn my life over to Him through His son Jesus Christ. I did just that, and I woke up feeling as if I was born again, no worries, no signs of depression. Just an innermost glow. I am now privileged to say I am a born again Christian. There has been a transformation, I am no longer aggressive, moody and arrogant; now I feel love happy, kind and generous.*

Yours

Mandy